PHL

54060000059179

WITHDRAWN

THE
PAUL HAMLYN
LIBRARY

DONATED BY
THE PAUL HAMLYN
FOUNDATION
TO THE
BRITISH MUSEUM

opened December 2000

D0310765

Food and Festivals
A Flavour of BRAZIL

Mariana Serra

WAYLAND

641.598 SER.

Other titles:

Cover photograph: A boy carries home a basket of vegetables from the market.

Title page: A boy dressed as one of the Candomblé gods.

Contents page: A dancer in colourful costume taking part in the June Festivals.

All Wayland books encourage children to read and help them improve their literacy.

✓ The contents page, page numbers, headings and index help locate specific pieces of information.

✓ The glossary reinforces alphabetic knowledge and extends vocabulary.

✓ The further information section suggests other books dealing with the same subject.

✓ Find out more about how this book is specifically relevant to the National Literacy Strategy on page 31.

First published in 1999 by Wayland Publishers Limited, 61 Western Road, Hove, East Sussex, BN3 1JD, England

© Copyright 1999 Wayland Publishers Limited

Series editor: Polly Goodman
Book editor: Alison Cooper
Designer: Tim Mayer

British Library Cataloguing in Publication Data
Serra, Mariana
  A Flavour of Brazil. – (Food and Festivals)
  1. Cookery, Brazilian – Juvenile literature 2. Festivals, Brazil – Juvenile literature 3. Food habits – Brazil – Juvenile literature 4. Brazil – Social life and customs – Juvenile literature
  I. Title II. Brazil
  641.5'981

ISBN 0 7502 2464 9

Typeset by Mayer Media
Printed and bound in Italy by EuroGrafica, Vicenza.

Find Wayland on the Internet at http://www.wayland.co.uk

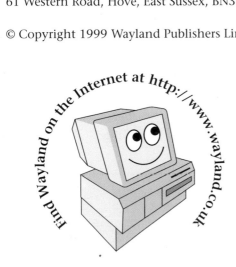

CONTENTS

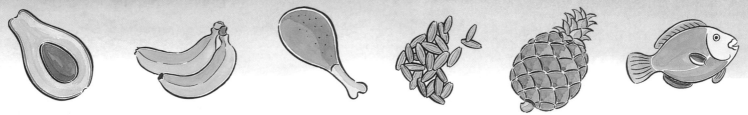

Brazil and its Food

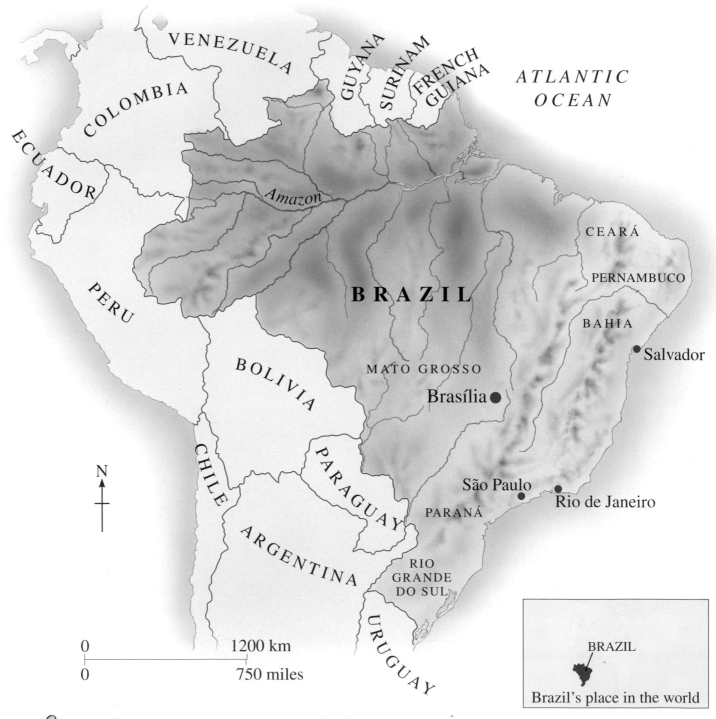

VENEZUELA

COLOMBIA

ECUADOR

GUYANA

SURINAM

FRENCH GUIANA

ATLANTIC OCEAN

Amazon

PERU

BRAZIL

CEARÁ

PERNAMBUCO

BAHIA

● Salvador

BOLIVIA

MATO GROSSO

Brasília ●

N

CHILE

PARAGUAY

São Paulo ●

● Rio de Janeiro

PARANÁ

ARGENTINA

RIO GRANDE DO SUL

URUGUAY

| 0 | | 1200 km |
| 0 | | 750 miles |

BRAZIL

Brazil's place in the world

BLACK BEANS AND RICE

Brazilians eat black beans and rice almost every day. These foods are very nutritious. *Feijoada* (pronounced fay-joo-ada) is a dish made with black beans.

FISH

Most Brazilians live near rivers or the coast, where they can find a delicious variety of seafood and fish. Tasty dishes such as the mimini fish shown here are popular.

CASSAVA

Cassava is a staple food in the rain forest in the north. You can see some on sale at the bottom of this picture. Throughout Brazil cassava is used in many sweet and savoury dishes.

SUGAR AND OIL

Sugar-cane is grown on plantations like the one in this picture. Oil for cooking is taken from palm trees. Sugar and oil are the main energy foods for people living in the dry north-east.

CATTLE, PIGS AND CHICKEN

Cattle, pigs and chickens are kept on big farms. Brazilians eat a lot of meat and barbecued meat is very popular.

FRUIT

Many exotic types of fruit, such as graviola and açaí, grow in the wild. Oranges, bananas and other fruits are grown on large plantations.

5

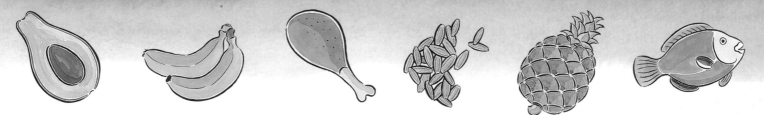

Food and Farming

Brazil is one of the largest countries in the world. It covers over half of the continent of South America. More than 165 million people live there.

In the north of Brazil lies the world's biggest rain forest, called the Amazon. The climate here is hot and wet. North-eastern Brazil is always hot and dry, almost like a desert. In Rio Grande do Sul, in the south, winters can be so cold that it sometimes snows.

▼ A farm worker with his children on a sugar-cane plantation in Pernambuco.

Rice and black beans

There are so many different climates in Brazil that a wide variety of crops can be grown there. Rice and black beans are the two staple foods. Black beans are grown anywhere where the weather is hot enough (except in the rain forest). Rice needs warm weather and wet soil, so it is grown in the swampy fields in western Brazil.

▲ These people in São Paulo are helping themselves to some *feijoada,* which is a favourite dish made with black beans.

◄ Farmers harvesting rice in western Brazil.

THE CASSAVA SECRET

Cassava is a vegetable that grows underground. Parts of the plant can be poisonous if eaten raw. The people of South America were the first to use cassava. When Europeans came to Brazil, the local people had to teach them how to cook cassava so that it was safe to eat.

▲This market stall in Ceará sells cassava, along with other fruit and vegetables.

Growing crops

Most fruits and vegetables come from very large plantations. These are found all over Brazil, except in the rain forest. It is difficult to grow crops in the rain forest. Rainforest peoples move from place to place, gathering plants that grow in the wild for food.

◀ A cowboy rounds up a herd of cattle in Mato Grosso.

▼ This man in Paraná is preparing *churrasco*.

Barbecues

Farmers in the west keep thousands of cattle on vast ranches. The huge herds have to be moved regularly to fresh grazing land.

Most Brazilians are great meat-lovers. The cowboys of the south, who are called *gaúchos* (pronounced gow-oo-chuss), say that they make the best barbecues in the world. They cover the large joints of meat in rock salt before they cook them, and the cooked meat is called *churrasco* (pronounced shur-hass-co).

◀ This girl is cooking turtles, traditional food among the peoples of the rain forest.

People and religions

The peoples of the rain forest were the first to live in Brazil. Some of their descendants still speak their traditional languages, and they have their own religious beliefs, too. But most Brazilians today are Catholics, and their language is Portuguese. This is because, in 1500, settlers from Portugal arrived in Brazil and ruled the country for more than 300 years.

The Portuguese settlers brought slaves from Africa to work on their plantations. The slaves had their own religious beliefs. As time passed, these beliefs became a faith called Candomblé.

Candomblé followers believe in many gods, who are called *orixás* (pronounced 'o-ree-shas'). In Brazil, it is quite normal to belong to more than one religion. Many Candomblé followers believe that their gods are the same as the Catholic saints, and most Catholics like to join in the non-Christian festivals.

This woman belongs ▶ to the Candomblé faith. She is selling traditional food from Bahia.

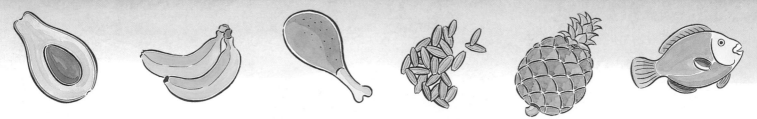

Carnaval

Carnival in Brazil is called *Carnaval*, and some people describe it as the biggest party in the world. Carnival began in Europe, hundreds of years ago. It was originally celebrated by Catholics. In Brazil today, it is enjoyed by people of all religions. Some of the most spectacular celebrations are held in Rio de Janeiro.

▼Children dressed up for *Carnaval* in Salvador.

Samba school parades

▲ A glittering *Carnaval* parade in Rio de Janeiro.

At *Carnaval* time the streets of Rio are filled with people dancing to the sound of the samba. Samba is a type of Brazilian music that uses drums to create a strong rhythm. It developed from the African music used in Candomblé ceremonies. During *Carnaval*, different samba schools hold colourful street parades. These last for four days (and nights!).

SAMBA SCHOOLS

Community groups known as samba schools spend all year preparing stunning costumes and dances for the official *Carnaval* parades. They compete against each other to see who can create the best costumes and music.

How *Carnaval* began

In the Middle Ages, Christians in Europe celebrated carnival in the days before Lent began. Lent is a period when it is traditional for Christians to go without meat, or even without any food at all. It is a way to remember the last days in the life of Jesus. Carnival was a time to eat a lot, drink a lot, and have a lot of fun before the fasting began. The Portuguese brought the carnival tradition to Brazil.

▲ These delicious fruits have been prepared for a *Carnaval* banquet.

ROYAL FOR A DAY

At the old European carnivals, kings, queens, lords and ladies would dress up as poor people to join in the festival. Their servants chose their own carnival kings and became royal for a day. In Brazil, African slaves were allowed a few days to party and make fun of their masters by dressing up as them.

Everywhere in Brazil, ▶ people take to the streets to dance and have fun during *Carnaval*.

The flavour of *Carnaval*

▲ Hot chillis add a spicy flavour to pepper-scented rice.

Most Brazilians no longer fast during Lent, but they still like to prepare special meals to celebrate *Carnaval*. Pepper-scented rice is a *Carnaval* favourite. It shows how the different cooking styles of the peoples who have come to live in Brazil have mingled together. Rice is popular in Portuguese cookery, and the spicy peppers show the African taste for hot foods.

Pepper-scented Rice

EQUIPMENT

Chopping board   Tablespoon
Sharp knife   Large saucepan
Measuring jug   Wooden spoon
Kettle

INGREDIENTS (for 2–3)

1 Tablespoon of vegetable oil
1 Small onion, finely diced
1 Garlic clove, minced
200 g Long-grain rice
1 Chilli pepper
450 ml of hot water
$\frac{1}{2}$ Teaspoon of salt

1 Pour the vegetable oil into the saucepan and heat it for a few seconds.

2 Add the onion, garlic and rice, and fry gently, stirring for about 4 minutes.

3 Add the chilli pepper, hot water and salt. Stir well and bring to the boil.

4 Simmer for 15–20 minutes. When the rice is quite soft and the water has gone, remove the pepper and serve.

Be careful when using knives and hot pans. Ask an adult to help you.

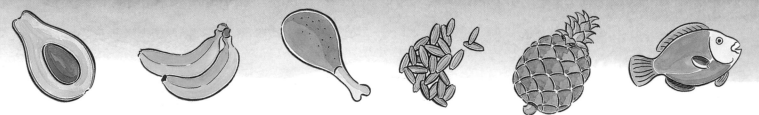

Bumbá Bull

The Bumbá Bull festival, or *Boi Bumbá,* is celebrated in many villages throughout the Amazon area. The celebrations are linked to an ancient rainforest legend. Some people travel long distances to celebrate the festival in the small village of Paratins. The journey by boat can last up to a week. At the village, they dress up in colourful costumes, and there is music, dancing and fireworks.

▼ A rainforest family in their village home near the Amazon river.

The legend of the Bumbá bull

The legend of the Bumbá bull tells of a pregnant woman who was having cravings for certain types of food. One day, her cravings got so bad that she asked her husband to kill his boss's prized bull.

When her husband's boss found out, he was very unhappy. He called the local *pajé*, who is the religious leader of the rainforest people. The *pajé* danced around the dead bull, casting spells. After much effort, he was able to bring the bull back to life, making everyone dance for joy.

These people are ► dressed up as the characters in the Bumbá bull legend.

Festival food

FISHING IN THE AMAZON

The traditional way for rainforest people to catch their fish is by standing in the river and catching the fish on a spear. This can be dangerous if piranhas come their way. Piranhas are fish with big teeth that can attack swimmers.

Because the man in the rainforest legend liked his bull so much, people avoid eating meat during the Bumbá Bull festival. Sometimes they have fish, which they catch in the Amazon river. There is a recipe for a fish dish on the opposite page. This recipe also uses coconut milk, which is a very popular ingredient in Brazilian cookery.

▼ Fish dishes such as mimini fish are very popular in Brazil.

Mimini fish

EQUIPMENT

Chopping board   Spatula
Sharp knife   Wooden spoon
Garlic crusher   Plate
Frying pan

INGREDIENTS (for 1)

100 g White fish
1 Tablespooon of vegetable oil
1 Medium onion, chopped
1 Clove of garlic, crushed
3 Tomatoes, chopped
Salt and pepper
400 ml Can of coconut milk or
1/2 packet of creamed coconut,
dissolved in 350 ml boiling water

Heat the oil in a large frying pan for a few seconds, add the fish and fry until golden. Put it on a plate and set it aside.

Fry the onions and garlic until soft.

Stir in the tomatoes and fry them for 3 minutes. Add a little salt and pepper.

Put the fried fish back in the pan and stir in the coconut milk. Bring the mixture to the boil. Serve immediately with rice.

Be careful when using knives and hot pans. Ask an adult to help you.

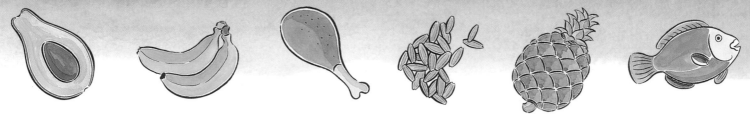

June Festivals

Catholic traditions are very important in Brazil. The June Festivals, or *Festas Juninas*, are held in honour of Saint Anthony, Saint Peter and Saint John. Saint John has the greatest number of followers, and all of them look forward to Saint John's Day, especially the children.

In parts of north-east Brazil, people believe that Saint John protects the harvest of sweetcorn and green beans, so they will all have plenty of food in the year ahead. Saint John's festival is celebrated when these crops are harvested.

▼ Harvesting sweetcorn in eastern Brazil.

Saint John's Day

Brazilian Catholics begin the holy day of Saint John by going to church for a special mass. At school, children listen to stories about the saint.

In the afternoon, outdoor parties begin. Everyone dresses up in the traditional clothes worn by the farm workers of central Brazil. People play traditional games, such as jumping over a bonfire or trying to climb up a slippery stick. It is a day of fun for everyone.

A dancer in traditional ▶ clothes at a Saint John's Day party.

23

At all the June Festivals, Brazilians like to eat food made from sweetcorn, the crop protected by Saint John. They use sweetcorn to make puddings and cakes, as well as eating it on the cob. You can find out how to make a delicious sweetcorn cake on the opposite page.

▲ Sweetcorn cake is a traditional Saint John's Day dish.

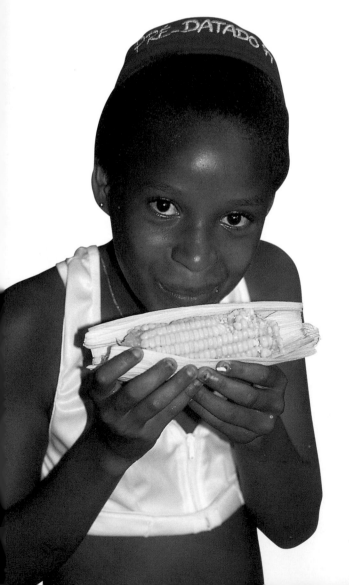

MUSIC FOR ALL

People enjoy listening and dancing to *forró* music at Saint John's Day parties. *Forró* music is played on accordions and percussion instruments. The word *Forró* comes from the time when the British came to Brazil to build the first railways. Every month, the British bosses invited the builders to a party that was open for all. 'For all' became *Forró*.

◄ A young girl enjoys a tasty corn on the cob.

Sweetcorn Cake

INGREDIENTS

325 g Can of sweetcorn, drained
100 g Butter, softened
125 g Wholemeal flour
3 Eggs, beaten
400 ml Can of coconut milk
1 Tablespoon of baking powder
400 g Caster sugar

EQUIPMENT

Tin opener
Food processor
  or bowl
Wooden spoon
  or spatula

Large greased
  loaf tin
Oven gloves
Wire rack

Set the oven to 180°C/Gas Mark 4. Put all the ingredients into a food processor or bowl and blend or mix until smooth.

Pour the mixture into the loaf tin.

Bake for approximately 50 minutes. To test if the cake is done, put a skewer into the centre – it should come out clean.

Turn the cake on to a wire rack to cool, then slice and serve.

Be careful when using the oven. Ask an adult to help you.

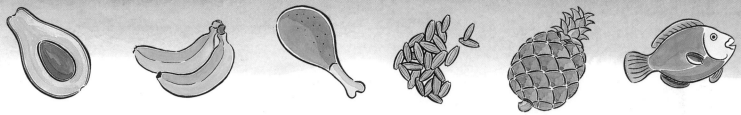

Bonfim

Salvador is the oldest city in Brazil, and the people who live there have kept the Candomblé religion alive. Festivals held in honour of the different gods, called *orixás,* are celebrated in Salvador throughout the year.

▼ Candomblé women in Bahia dress in white to honour the god Oxalá.

The *Bonfim* festival in January honours the god Oxalá, father of all *orixás.* Many Brazilians say that Oxalá is the same as Jesus Christ. White roses are Oxalá's favourite flowers, and black beans are his favourite food.

THE *ORIXAS*

Oxalá is linked with Jesus Christ, and the other *orixás* are linked with Christian saints. Each *orixá* has a favourite food, too.

Orixá	Christian saint	Favourite food
Ogum	St Anthony	Yam
Oxóssi	St George	Corn with coconut
Oxumaré	St Bartholomew	Beans with corn and palm oil.

Candomblé followers dress in white for the *Bonfim* festival, as a symbol of peace and purity.

Thousands of people join in a procession to the Church of Our Lord Jesus of *Bonfim*. There, they watch some of the Candomblé women wash the steps outside the church with rose water.

Later, people have fun dancing to traditional Candomblé music for many hours.

These Bahia women ▶ are taking part in the ceremony of washing the church steps, like the one that takes place at *Bonfim*.

BONFIM RIBBONS

Many Brazilians believe that ribbons bought in Salvador are lucky. According to tradition, if you wear the ribbons on your wrist until they break, three wishes will come true.

Oxalá's market

▲ These colourful *Bonfim* ribbons are believed to be lucky.

Near the *Bonfim* church, Candomblé women called *Bahianas* set up market stalls. The traditional goods on sale include *Bonfim* lucky ribbons and the black bean soup that is Oxalá's favourite food. There is a recipe for black bean soup on the opposite page.

▼ Black beans are used in a variety of dishes, including this tasty soup.

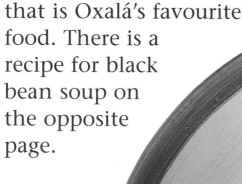

Black Bean Soup

EQUIPMENT

Chopping board	Can opener
Sharp knife	Ladle
Saucepan	Food processor

This recipe can also be made without a food processor – see Step 3.

INGREDIENTS (for 2–3)

250 g South American black beans, or dried kidney beans, soaked overnight

1 Onion, chopped

1 Garlic clove, chopped

1 Can of chopped tomatoes

1 Pork, chicken or vegetable stock cube

1 Tablespoon of chopped parsley

1 Tablespoon of chopped coriander

Put the beans in a saucepan, cover them with cold water and boil them for <u>at least ten minutes,</u> with the lid partially covering the pan.

Crumble the stock cube into the pan and add the other ingredients. Put on the lid and simmer for 15–20 minutes. Add more water if necessary.

Ladle the mixture into a food processor and blend until smooth, or simmer for another 10 minutes.

Pour the soup back into the pan and reheat. Serve with crispy bacon sprinkled on the top.

Be careful when using hot pans and knives. Ask an adult to help you.

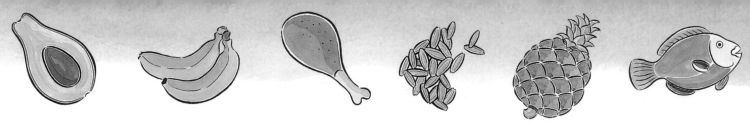

Glossary

Accordions Instruments that are played by squeezing an air bag in and out and pressing keys on a keyboard.

Catholics Christians who are led by the Pope in Rome, Italy.

Climate The type of weather that an area usually has.

Cravings Very strong feelings of needing something, such as a certain type of food.

Descendants Relatives of people who died a long time ago.

Fast To go without food or without certain foods.

Mass An important Catholic ceremony.

Nutritious Full of nutrients, the parts of foods that help our bodies to grow and stay healthy.

Plantations Large farms where crops are grown, usually so that they can be sold to other countries.

Rain forest Thick forest that grows in areas where the climate is hot and wet.

Ranches Large farms where animals, especially cattle, are kept.

Settlers People who travelled from one country to live in another country.

Slaves People who are owned by other people. They are not paid for their work and have no freedom.

Staple foods Foods that are the main part of people's everyday diet.

Swampy Wet. A swamp is an area of very wet land, sometimes thickly covered with plants.

Picture acknowledgements

Chapel Studios/Zul Mukhida 5 (top right), 16, 20, 24 (top), 28 (bottom); Sue Cunningham *Cover*, Title page, contents page, 9 (bottom), 12, 13, 14, 18, 19, 23, 24 (bottom), 27, 28 (top); Eye Ubiquitous/James Davis 11; Hutchison 26; Impact 22/Marco Siqueira; Panos 7 (bottom)/Sean Sprague; Edward Parker 5 (centre right), 5 (bottom left), 6, 9 (top), 10; South American Pictures 5 (top left)/Jason P. Howe, 5 (centre left)/Tony Morrison, 7 (top)/Jason P. Howe, 8/Tony Morrison, 15/Tony Morrison; Wayland Picture Library/Julia Waterlow 5 (bottom right).

Fruit and vegetable artwork is by Tina Barber. The map on page 4 is by Peter Bull and Hardlines. The step-by-step artwork is by Judy Stevens.

Topic Web and Resources

GEOGRAPHY
Locality study.

Weather.

Farming and how land is used.

Comparing physical landscapes.

MATHS
Use and understand data and measures (recipes).

Use and understand fractions.

Use and read measuring instruments: scales.

SCIENCE
Food and nutrition.

Plants in different habitats.

Separating mixtures of materials: sieving.

Changing materials through heat.

Food & Festivals
TOPIC WEB

HISTORY
Colonialism.

DESIGN AND TECHNOLOGY
Design a costume for *Carnaval*.

Make a bull mask.

ENGLISH
Make up a story or poem about *Carnaval*.

Write a slogan to sell a Brazilian speciality, e.g. black bean soup.

MODERN FOREIGN LANGUAGES
Everyday activities: food.

People, places and customs.

MUSIC
Listen to samba music.

BOOKS TO READ

Country Insights: Brazil by Marion Morrison (Wayland, 1996)

Discovering Brazil by Marion Morrison (Zoe Books, 1996)

We Come From Brazil by André Lichtenberg (Wayland, 1999)

USEFUL ADDRESSES

Brazilian Embassy, 32 Green Street, London W1Y 4AT

Hispanic and Luso-Brazilian Council, Canning House, 2 Belgrave Square, London SW1X 8PJ

This book meets the following specific objectives of the National Literacy Strategy's Framework for Teaching:

✔ Range of work in non-fiction: simple recipes (especially Year 2, Term 1), instructions, labels, captions, lists, glossary, index.

✔ Vocabulary extension: words linked to particular topics (food words) and technical words from work in other subjects (geography and food science).

Index

Page numbers in **bold** mean there is a photograph on the page.